Universal
Reflections

by
Nathaniel Brooks, Jr., M.D.

Eggman Publishing
Nashville, Tennessee

ISBN: 1-886371-53-9

Cover Design: Charles Hooper

Eggman Publishing
3012 Hedrick Street
Nashville, TN 37203

For interviews and other information, call
615-386-0133
800-396-4626

ACKNOWLEDGMENTS

My thanks to the entire staff and consultants of Eggman Publishing. Special thanks to Stephanie Glenn, Kathy McAndrew, and Cynthia Meredith. I also extend my thanks to Stephen W. Johnson, and to Dean Walker, who contributed to the original cover design of the book.

Being raised in a very large family has indeed left its pleasant memorable impressions. The possibility of listing everyone is endless. Therefore, I would like to take this opportunity to thank a host of many brothers, sisters, aunts, uncles, cousins, nephews, nieces, and in-laws, for without you all I would have missed out on the most important common thread that binds humanity—family.

To my mother and father, I thank you for the many ways you have inspired me to work hard and excel.

To my mother- and father-in-law, thank you for the kind advice and joyful moments shared over the many years.

Above all, I wish to thank the many readers who seek the best life has to offer and are willing to share their many encounters in a positive manner with all humanity.

DEDICATION

My humble thanks to many friends and family very dear
to my heart, for their love and kindness has enriched the
words within this collection for all humanity. There are
countless names and faces which pleasantly bring a smile
as I reflect upon many years of generosity. To all, I kindly
send my warmest regards through the words found
within...

To Paulette, my loving wife, my deepest gratitude
in being blessed with your warm presence. To Nathaniel
III and Tashaunda, our son and daughter, your gentle
presence has been a wonderful source of joy and happiness
we have shared together on this journey.

TABLE OF CONTENTS

Universal
Reflections

THE EUCHARIST

Reaching out into the distant space of unfilled void
The Creator formed the planets and stars eternally.
And from the frozen depths and molten dust vastness
    beyond
Molded the divinity of oneness with enduring diversity.

Then the Creator rested on the final day
Last memories thence was of innocence at play.
The entire universe smiled with warmth
That emanates from the birth of a child.

The sea of tranquility remained an endless refuge
Where all creatures existed in peaceful harmony.
And scattered amongst the many stars and planets
Were the abundance which provided sustenance for life.

Creation's children were entrusted as caretakers.
In time they separated themselves by uncommon beliefs.
The Eucharist became lost in the casting shadows
Of worldly battles fought for possessions of flesh and
    soul.

Then from the body of creation a bright form appeared
As the great son of everlasting salvation.
The redeeming light filled the void of lost hope, misery,
    and despair.
And those entering the light witnessed spiritual
    fulfillment of the universe.

EVERLASTING

Centuries of old beckons to time
Years unfold mere one so fine.
Days pass with the speed of life
And moonlight nights cast vivid shadows
    O' beauty seen by light.

The hours have watched you well, my dear,
With circumspect eyes.
Your song, dance, and laughter too,
Awakens lifeless spirits as no others do.

The minutes have mirrored your every move.
With second reflections fleeting, an essence veiled,
    remains,
And adorned by spirits of visions foretold
This moment seeks your ageless grace to behold.

UNVEILING INTERLUDE

As a humble priest walked through the serene temple in silence, an image appeared.
And the priest asked,
"Who are you ?"
And the image spoke,
"I am Iknabb from the land of Tanruor."
"And what is your purpose for your being here at Zseczon?"
Iknabb replied,
"I have no purpose. I drift with the clouds and blend with the currents of the sea."
"Ah, my dear, you have travelled all this distance, yet, having no purpose, you enter the land of Zseczon. Is that not purpose in itself?"
"What do you mean, priest?"
And, he answered,
"I say to you Iknabb, is not the purpose written in the will of destiny? Has not destiny brought you through these gates from your land of Tanruor?"
"Yes, I am here," replied Iknabb, "but I know not of this thing called destiny, as my bringer."
The priest replied,
"You drift with the clouds and blend with currents of the sea, yet you know not of your destiny nor purpose in thee. Be not which is not of thee. Acknowledge that which encounters thee. Here you will find purpose and destiny."

CREATION'S DREAMS

A person without dreams is a person without purpose nor destination.

Beyond the limits of thy talents lies
a hidden fountain of even greater creativity.

ARABIAN WOMEN

In the distant horizon beyond pristine mountains,
trade-wind seas, and cool valley streams there
flourishes The Desert Flower. With each breath of
fresh air there drifts enticing fragrances drawing me
closer to her sensuous veils. From the body of her
floral oasis glows quiescent tones as the sun at early
light dawn. And the dew upon her petals sparkles as
the stars at night just before twilight morn. Within
the warm innocence of her dark exotic eyes there
shines the eternal spark that kindles love's flame in
my heart. As she dances the love song and passion
desire burns, her blooms withers the call for loves
caressing embrace.

IN REQUEST FOR ARMED PEACE

A country in captivity wanting not war
Seek nations of many diplomacy cries.
A kingdom in exile, a tyrants resolve
Denials of peace resolutions defied.

As grey island fortresses sail mine-full seas
Launch guided hawks to targets afar
Along paths so chosen by greed blind destiny
Strikes sighted prey through satellite eye stars.

As missiles in flight dance destructions duel at night
And soaring birds with rays shield stalking tanks.
The tracks so weaved across barren land
Leads to the place valor met victory in the sand.

As we stand upon ancient ground
With desert sand beneath our feet.
A tactical force ever so swift
The task before us, never retreat.

An armada forged with the courage of steel
Charged onward through ancient battlefields,
Engaged the enemy with a thunderous roar
Until rocket and cannon fire was no more.

As the sound of silence pierced the air
And mortal wounded laid in fear.
The victims of war, now in defeat
Captives by fate providers of peace.

A country war-scarred, sea-cloud's black rain
Restores the kingdom in exile to rule again.
As soldiers of war return to distant lands
Lives so honored through peace victories stand.

THE ART OF MEDICAL MAGIC

It is taught in medical, nursing, and many specialty
  schools,
Lessons learned conforms to individual patients rules.
And ample dose of healing elixirs given
Is proportional to caring feeling not hidden.

Therapy rendered is more than medical knowledge
  acquired
Rather, in dedication, work, and true hearts desire.
The healing process takes place beyond the wound site
At a place which harbors loves meaning to life.

As the chosen practitioner of this ancient art
Treat the patient within from the very start.
And, if the performance does not go well this day,
Be not discouraged by rigors that often dismay.

Within the magical chest one will often find
A warm heart's touch explaining complex matters in
    kind.
No trick of the trade can exceed that of simple hope
When matched with the human instrument as your
    caring scope.

Patience are wise mentors with worldly healing skills
That attends with gentle hands strengthened through
    perseverance will.
So wear proudly the medical garments of humor, care,
    and concern.
Now wave the magician's wand that glitters love with
    each kind act in turn.

ZEN

The total universe is God's temple and everything within is sacred.

To reap life's benefits one must learn to interpret its many moods as a force which perpetuates our existence.

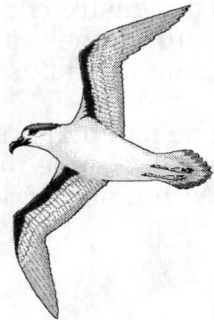

PATHS OF ADVERSITY

Found among ruins of the ancient shrine
There appeared a sage reading verses from the lost scribe
To those that fell subject to the great famine
Of the human spirit.
From a calm voice these words were spoken.

The ears that attentively listens today
Are the receptacles by which the minds of tomorrow
Accepts change.

The voice that speaks hate with passion and desire
Also possesses gentle sounds that call for peace
In times of turmoil.

The eyes that was once blind to the sight of hope
Are the same that envision the needs of many
Through the spectacles of present time.

The outstretched hands accepting food for mere survival
Returns the gratitude with gifts reaped
From the fields of human generosity.

The feet that once walked the roads to self-destruction
Are the same that travel the paths of adversity
With inner pride, purpose, and success.

SOLACE

It is through giving even a small portion of love
We receive the greater gift of living in return.

Through acceptance of our many human qualities
We find humor in our most imperfect moments.

Through seeking divine harmony within
We are enlightened to supreme harmony of our universe.

Through material greed of the flesh
We disrupt daily blessings bestowed upon us.

Through simple pleasures of togetherness
Loneliness remains a stranger to the house of joy.

Through the birth of each spiritual island
We endure as sanctuaries of living hope.

QUINTESSENCE

I have looked beyond the color of skin
And heard melodies of hearts lovers often sing
Sharing simple pleasures of joy happiness often brings.

I have looked beyond the color skin
Into eyes wisdom stories told
And reaped such treasures beyond
'Twas greater than worldly gold.

I have looked beyond the color of skin
And beheld that truth was never blind
To past, present, nor future time.

I have looked beyond the color of skin
To find the infant child reaching out
With warmth of a simple hug, pure and whole,
Summoned angels above to lift my very soul.

RESOURCEFUL LIVING

A gift presented without true expression from the heart is
   as offering a cup without water and expecting the
   thirsty to drink.

For every life on earth there is a purpose for its existence.
For every breath we take and bold step we make
Along the many roads we travel to places we've never
   known
There is none more important than the road
That returns us to the peaceful solitude
Of our own self awareness and purpose found within.

WINDS OF TIME

Wisdom enters through the gates of age and time.

*And Youth rides high on spirited wings
of zestful living.*

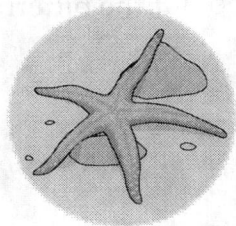

PHASE IV

When born,
    Life was a gift
    Death, surely a promise.
    With no more to say
    But a weeping cry
    I, damned by my parents
    Was left to die.
    But mother earth
    Seeing fit I survive
    My worthless birth
    Took me in as her own
    And prepared me for life's dangers
    In my unwelcoming home.

In youth,
    Tossed and driven into life's
    Pitfall dangers
    Not fear of death I now face
    But the bitterness of life I now taste.

Confused by thoughts of
   Survival in my mind
   I sought help from
   Mother Nature so kind
   Who took me in as her own
   Anointed my wounds
   With sacred herbs to heal
   Ages of scares and scorns.

Now old,
   Though tired and worn
   Wishes of eternal life steadily grows strong.
   I've witnessed earth's miraculous changes
   In this vast universe
   And survived life's many dangers
   Since early birth.
   Once again I turned to mother earth
   In hope of escape.
   Sensing my plea for rebirth,
   She opened wide her glorious gates,
   And with outstretched arms of welcome
   I humbly cuddled into the warmth of her essence.

IMPOVERISHED CHILDHOOD MEMORIES

In the city I feel the pulse and rhythm beat
Of existing in the Ghetto where drugs rule the streets.

In the community of people with senseless negligent care
A neighborhood passiveness replaces action with hidden
    fear.

In the clouded crack houses where lost souls are always
    found
Idle minds remain silently wasted with trash poverty
    abounds.

In this place called home, my family cries with sudden
    rage
Trapped in the urban jungle entangled social cage.

In the park, crystal powder so white is sold at black
    market's daily price
While supplies from white castles remain legally fortified
    distantly out of site.

In the corner store I tried to buy a loaf of bread
Some men came in I knew, and shot the owner dead.

The scars from the streets I walk dwell constantly in my
    head.
Dream terrors wake me up at night—bleeding color red.

The violence that surrounds me creates this pain I feel
Please somebody help me survive this horrible ordeal.

SERENITY

As the forest passes through changes of its leafy hue, so must we pass through our dormant, yet, not stagnant stage of spiritual awakening which harkens to the calls of revelations.

Even though, it is most easy to capitulate to the superficial barren dust that stirs about us. The difficulty lies in seeking out the form from whence the dust came. Should you ever find it, embrace the essence with true arms of uncompromising love.

UNIVERSE CITY

We attend the school of life
     For nature is our teacher.
We belong to the commune of humanity
     Their welfare is our concern.
Our home is the planet earth
     Its natural resources we must preserve.
We believe in the great spirit
     For faith will guide and deliver us.
We have studied ancient civilizations,
     Modern arts, and the sciences
But long for what the future beholds.

We have challenged the inner fortitude of our very soul
     And tapped a minuscule part of those powers which
     lie within.
We have seen visionary ideas which stagger the
          imagination
     Only to be reminded of our quest for knowledge.
We are temporary residents of this universe
     A space occupied by spirit will.
We must leave now so that others may take our place.
     They, too, will become fertile ground for the seeds of
          knowledge.
And, the fruits they bear shall in spirit live.

I, GIVEN

I, given knowledge;
    the uneducated I must teach.
I, given wisdom;
    the foolish I must seek
    To help them perform life's needy feats.
I, given strength;
    the sick I must help,
    To ease the agony of pain they've so often felt.

I, given life;
    Only not care or,
    To win all human strife?
I, given so little time
    To work wonders for all mankind.
I, to suffer hardships all men bear.

MY BELOVED

We first wept as we looked beyond ourselves towards a place where lonely hearts reconcile. Our spirits touched as we became one. We then found ourselves in celestial clouds where friendship lights the way. Never parting from that day, we shared love through living and received life through giving. In the place peace often rests, I will always be waiting where our hearts first met.

POETRY

Poetry is an expression of feelings when communicated, whether verbal or written, can be interpreted in many different ways according to one's dynamic life experiences.

THE GATHERING

A place where kinfolk of all humanities
Bond as one to travel life's eternal roads
A time to wave the banner of family unity
To skies above where four winds blow.

A place where hearts in family bondage gather
In midst of harvest fields, on peaceful mountain sides
On the urban avenues of life, upon banks where rivers
    run wide
To share the love and joy kinship readily provides.

A place where mother earth and father sky
Join to celebrate the days of spiritual living
Through pleasant memories of past years gone by
With words of honored truth from hearts freely giving.

A place where the vigor of youth and wisdom of ages
Carry on conversations whispered by voices of creation.
A time when family togetherness rekindles lights of hope
That shines brightly for children of all generations.

A place in time where the grand greatness of humanity
Runs through our veins, exists with triumphant purpose
And survives proudly within us all.

FAITH

From birth, we all are endowed with special gifts
Which lie dormant within the caverns of creativity.
Within the deepest recesses there exist renewing springs
Which nourishes our yearning for spiritual awakening.

For some, a life filled with seasonal changes
May leave such treasures buried among the ruins of lost
    hopelessness.
For others, they blindly search by day into the emptiness
    of the night.
Be not afraid of the distant darkness, for the light of
    revelation is upon you.
You are not alone in the barren desert of despair,
For in this most desolate place, you will find the springs
    for which you have searched.
Belief alone has brought you thus far, thirst not any
    longer.
Impart the sand from beneath your feet, a fountain will
    eternally flow.
Welcome to this resourceful oasis.
Here, sip from the chalice of faith.

INTROSPECTION

Knowledge is knowing those things one professes to know and searching for those things that one does not know.

The being found within the body of truth is among the purest form of universal enlightenment.

RECEIVING

A true gift is given only when self gratification of giving is received in return.

COMPASSIONATE

To give a beggar a penny, nickel, or dime is, at times, not really what he asks for. It is better to give of thyself—compassionate wisdom to help the beggar forevermore.

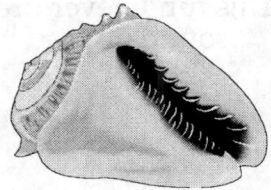

A FUN WORLD

Run, run, skip, jump on streets and dusty roads
Squirt-water wars, cardboard shields, and tree-stick
    swords
Enter the child's fun-filled world, dizzy spinning twirls
Of laughter, fun, and make-believe of little boys and
    girls

Hopscotch, slip shots, having fun on summer's day
Marble rings, pebble slings, games we often play
Mud-pie cakes, sunny-baked, Johnny took but never ate
Box-car races down the hill outrunning four-wheel skates

Ah! A strawberry, watermelon, or blackberry patch.
Yummy taste Mom's pies can surely match
Oh! Oh! A water-filled balloon got me wet
Laughter from above, I'm gonna tell Dad, you can bet.

Let's play pick-up sticks and bounce balls with paddle
    bats
And wish a genie takes us away on a magic carpet mat
Skip a rope, quicken strokes, my feet barely touch the
    ground
This fun I never tire of, I hope the dinner bell never
    sounds

Dress me up in Mom's best old stuff
Hat, purse, and lacy dress skirt
Playhouse tea, a party just for me
In a world of doll friends and children's fantasy

Spinning tops and yo yo drops dance across the floor
Treehouse guests for me knock knock on the door
My brother wants to play comic book heroes, I don't
    know what for
Having fun till we slump and sleep brings sweet dreams
    for evermore.

SURVIVAL

The true test of character lies in one's action under strenuous conditions.

A FLOWER BLOOMS

I have only one ambition in life.
That is, to live it fruitfully in hope to reseed the
universe the day I die.

BEING HUMAN

Acknowledgement of one's mistake is the foundation upon which one builds self-confidence and esteem.

REVEALING THE SOUL

The totality of mankind's action lies between two mundane virtues: one clothed in the garments of materialism and the other stands stark naked in the eyes of dignity.

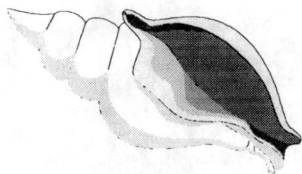

IN PASSING

Throughout this wakeful journey
She touched us with all her heart.
Rising at dawn to greet each morning
She tried to do her part.

Throughout this wakeful journey
She watched bright stars by night.
Letting each represent a friend in her life.

Throughout this wakeful journey
God charted her steady course.
Brought her through rough seas of hardship
Been her strength and source.

Throughout this wakeful journey
In passing through heaven's gate
She left us vivid memories of her strong-fast faith.

ABORTUS

Unseen faces, unsung voices, unshed tears
Created by Races of those who bare.
Floating in protective seas of humanity
Destined for that which is not to be.

Aging in crypts of bodily changes.
These are not wombs of just mere strangers.
Yet lurks threats of undecided dangers.

A smile, a tear, emotions to wear
On faces of Races of those who care.
A voice, a song, few words to sing
From fragile ones who dare to belong.

CITIZEN

I am the conscience of government
A minute, yet inseparable part.
My actions format the institution of laws,
Dissemination of justice
And protection of inalienable rights for all.
In bearing these ideals through my actions,
And my actions alone, the spirit of freedom
    survives.

BLESSED GIVING

*The mere willingness to help can extend one's
potential far beyond perceived capabilities.*

SEEKING A SPIRITUAL FRIEND

It was not until I greeted life as a friend,
I found love within.

ON WAR

*The eventual success of a battle plan lies in the
tactical vision of the planner, the vision imparted,
and the planned execution under variable conditions.*

BLESSED PASSAGE

*Loss of life humbles one's consciousness
to the graces of the universe.*

CATHEDRAL OF PRAISE

*The cathedral of praise is more than just a
structure. It is a place in our hearts
which houses our spirit.*

TO "LOVE"

Loving is understanding.
Loving is sweetness of one's care.
Loving is simply existing
For you, "LOVE," even though we're
So far apart yet so near.

Loving is a need for giving.
Loving is the happiness of living.
Loving is cherishing the one you love true,
For moments shared are yet too few.

Loving is living through hardships and heartbreaks.
Loving is conquering life's little give and takes.
Loving is loving purely for the sake of love.
Love is a heart that can truly offer and accept love.

Loving is the mergence of body and soul,
A majestic touch of tranquil charm
And love, a course unchartered, harmoniously
    unfolds.
Loving is looking back on those tender years,
Or maybe a split second of happiness shared.
And saying, "Loving you was enough, my dear."

AS YOU ARE

Do not change your ways.
Through the years together your smile has cheered my
    days.
From the moment I first saw you
Emotions uttered feelings love could only say.

Do not change your ways.
When friends that last have long since passed
And life no longer holds me dear to you on this
    remembered day
Love will come to comfort you in a very special way.

So let your heart accept this gift life sends your way.
Keep your warm and tender smile
But do not change your ways.

LIVING TODAY

Life is more than just existing day by day.
Life is living with zest, zeal, and flair in
each and every way.

*Life is a massive form of countless changes.
Our ability to survive depends on our ability
to adapt to those changes.*

A BEDOUIN'S JOURNEY

We will never be the same again
For the winds of war has changed
The fertile land within our hearts
Which nourishes the seeds of hope.
We will never be the same again.

For the drought of despair continues to ravage
The land that war has robbed.
The pains and scars inflicted on our daily dreams.
Now obscures faint visions as the blackness of the night.
We will never be the same again.

For we hear the voices of many
But only understand the language of the desert.
We have travelled this land many times before in
    brethren caravans.
But this journey across our homeland
Has been an unfamiliar one with painful sorrow
For we are Bedouins from the desert of old.
We will never be the same again.

For our hearts were misled into the temple of false
    pillars.
The dwellings erected there of sand and stone
Were laden of mortar reaped from earth's precious
    reserves.
It was here we battled the true tyranny of our own
    deception.
We will never be the same again.

For then blew the storm from the North and East.
Upon her winds came harbingers called peace.
Within the eyes of those that seek
Praises to Allah in solitudes voice speak.
We will never be the same again.

For we feel the coldness of humane separation
And in the midst of desert heat
Our spirits thirst for the cleansing reign
A new ruler will bring again.
We will never be the same again.

For the clothing of human servitude is worn
We ask only for the sparse fabrics of humility.
Our feet are bare. We wish for sandals
To walk the roads of friendship.
We are tired of war and our bodies weary
We wish to rest in the light of peace once more.

COURAGE

An important part of our daily lives
Deals with turning adversities and
Disappointments into triumphs.
It is through our inner peace,
We accomplish our greatest feats.
May your inner peace strengthen you!

AN EMOTIONAL RETREAT

The eyes and ears are the receptacles through which the heart's emotions are expressed by hands of the poetical soul.

SIMPLICITY

In our most hurried moments, when our bare feet touch solid ground, let us not forget to feel the fine grains of sand, dew upon blades of grass, and the texture of sculptured boulders beneath our feet. May our pace so slow that we hear whispers of the wind, feel the misty rain and the warmth of the sun's radiant glow. In these simple pleasures there is more than enough for which we can be thankful.

SHOWERING SUNSHINE

Be thankful for the happy and sad times. To wish one without the other is to rob life of its two most cherished emotions—the tears of sadness and laughter of happiness.

ENDLESS JOURNEY

Living is a faithful walk through life
A simple measure of worthiness
Touching those we meet along the way.

Love is life's most precious gift
To be cherished, held gently
And nourished with trusting companionship.

Along the journey one will greet many strangers.
Here are a few loyal friends
To guide you even on the darkest day

It is Through giving, we receive.
Through courage, we conquer fear.
Through selfless action, honor bestowed.
Through seeking, destiny encountered.
Through love, hate perishes.
Through prayer and meditation
The spirit soars to peaceful solitude.

CHALLENGE

There shall be times when one will say
I have learned
Times when the walls of burden
Will stand stern
But only strength and wisdom
Will send them asunder
Times when one will say "I can't do"
And the task seems impossible until done.
Times when one will say
"I've done my best—
Challenged the test."
Times when your job will be done.
Life's long battle, you've won.

CRYPTIC INJUSTICE

Our native spoken language fell upon vengeful ears
Which harbored ill feelings; tragedies of distant wars
We were blamed for acts committed by those that came
    before.

Today our eyes met on a crowded street.
My appearance was ragged and sparsely poor.
I reached out my hand to greet a close friend
My heart once knew.
In return, a cold stare froze gestures
From a moment of human shame
Within the open shelter of the homeless.

In anger I called you many disrespectful words
Degraded myself within by thoughts silent
    consciousness only heard.

You clutched your purse when we came near
We meant no harm, being not aware
Of biased thoughts entrenched guarded fears.

I applied for a job for which no other applicant was better
    qualified.
But, many excuses were implied to this willing laborer
    denied.

Today another life was given unto me.
I chose an unfamiliar face called tomorrow
To raise the child my arms did not embrace.

The ideals by which we live are the foundations of our
    culture.
But whispers along the back hallway corridors
Silenced freedoms choice through judgments
Rooted in blind social ignorance.
In just this, through our actions, we perpetuate
Cryptic views witnessed by the eyes of colored
    indifference.

ENCHANTING MOMENT

With tranquil winds from long lost times swirling to and fro, our enchanted beings we merged with prevailing tones of our existence. In solitude, we quivered, not of fear, but of happiness we share. And opening our eyes we saw the light across the darkness of the sea. With ebbs washing our feet immaculately in the presence of purity and as gentle breezes convey fragrances from tall grasses on shore, we sighed in sheer delight. Just as the grasses harken to calls of the wind so shall we come as humble servants in thee to the end.

LAST BREATH

As we were drowning in the sea of life struggling to stay alive. My last breath I held in search for you only to revive.

YOUTH OF AGES

There is a place in the heart of our universe
A place where human growth has no boundaries
A place where the hands of time elevate the spirit,
Sharpens the mind, and strengthens the soul
To endure the wonder of it all.

There is a place in the heart of our universe
A place where tiny beings are shaped
By the gentle fingers of Life's many encounters.
A place where natural beauty has not, yet, been shrouded
In false pretenses of expectation, deception, and deceit.

There is a place in the heart of our universe
A place where the innocence of humanity
Remains pure as the falling rain, exists with triumphed
    laughter
And mends wounds today with pleasant thoughts of
    tomorrow.
A place where friendship speaks softly with wisdom,
kindness, and gratitude.

There is a place in the heart of our universe
A place where dreams are the chartered vessels to reality
And imagination the raw fuel that provides perpetual
    energy
For exploration to the outer limits of new discoveries.
A place where the heart touches what the eyes cannot
    see.

There is a place in the heart of our universe
A place where the youth of ages gather to celebrate the
    days living.
This place will always exist within the vast commune of
    life
As we allow the child of many seasons the joy of passing
Through the heart of our universe.

LIVING THROUGH TOMORROW

To understand death one must realize that death is intimately woven into the blanket of life; and the blanket of life warms our hearts with love.

Be not saddened by the occurrence of death; for it is only life giving rise to life once more.

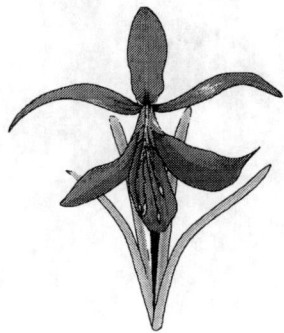

DESTINY

Success is more than a moment's fleeting thought. It is a way of life; a combination of many positive ideas placed in action to bring harmony and balance to the world in which we live. May the inner strength of our collective actions continue our success.

AWAKENING

To fear life is to fear one self.

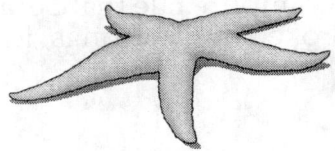

ABUNDANT GIFTS

Oh how we love the abundant gifts life has given us
Crystal springs, songs birds sing, we need not make a
    fuss
A glimmer of hope when we need it most
To climb life's most challenging slopes

Oh how we love the abundant gifts life has given us
Places well-known, joyously called home, we need not
    make a fuss
Warm summer days, sweet springs we say announced by
    floral hues
The call of fall's vibrant leaves summons winter's
magnificent views

Oh how we love the abundant gifts life has given us
Quaint nature trails, oceans to sail, we need not make a
    fuss
Lakes to swim at a moment's whim revive a weary soul
Youthful smiles throughout our lives lift spirits that
never grow old

Oh how we love the abundant gifts life has given us
Canoeing trips, splashing flips, we need not make a fuss
A campfire tale that became big as a whale
Broke lines and rings, in laughter we never fail

Oh how we love the abundant gifts life has given us
Bountiful grains, refreshing rains, we need not make a
    fuss
Succulent fruits, nourishing roots strengthen bodies we
    bare
Produced by life's flourishing gardens distantly far and
    near

Oh how we love the abundant gifts life has given us
A solo flight into the night, we need not make a fuss
A dreamy moon that glows across rolling moors
Casts star- gazers' light, illuminates bright distant shores

Oh how we love the abundant gifts life has given us
The arrival of a child to hold for a while, we need not
    make a fuss
A companion friend to the end ever present from dawn
    to dusk
Oh how we reap such abundant gifts life has in store for
    us.

AN ADVENTURE

In all events of human endeavor we encounter adversity due to dynamic change. As we take the high road to success, remember, we all possess the keys to unlock the door to our future. Use the many keys of faith, humor, kindness, and courage to open the doors of hope for all humanity.

NEW HORIZONS

The earth is not a crowded place.
There is room for all to roam.
We need not look very far
To find gentle creatures we so dearly are.

TRANSFORMATION

I have found a most powerful natural resource, for it lies within me. Now, let me seek the many ways I can express the true potential of my creative being.

PEACEFUL BEGINNING

Total exhaustion of one's physical being allows peaceful will yielding to spiritual fulfillment.

ETERNAL MERGENCE

Each heartbeat brings us closer
Within the rhythmic flow
Of universal harmony
Through love's endless passion glow

We will always be together
As the day transcends the night
For each breath we take as one
Our spirits soars the eternal heights

And no matter how far the parting
Of our physical being exist
Or length of time
Our separation may persist.

Never shall any force separate us
Not even beyond life.

CELESTIAL COMPANION

When I fail to rise in early morn
To greet the sunrise each splendid day
I miss the presence of being reborn
The blessings heaven sends my way.

When I feel the warmth of radiant stars
As they shine to light my way
I think of the many friends afar
And their smiles that brightens my every day.

When I meet new challenges that lie before me
As I traverse the great corridors of life
I know I'm not alone, you see,
'Cause God provides special armor through prayer
To overcome each little strife.

MAGNIFICENT WONDER

Earth
  Too enormous for one to possess it all
  Yet, through the hands of human servitude
  We hold the offerings humility brings
  To the table of universal needs

Earth
  Too vast for one mind to learn all its secrets
  Yet, we possess the capacity to harness
  Its many teachings far beyond
  That which simple logic can never explain

Earth
  Too great for the mightiest army to conquer its
    purpose
  Yet, we find resourceful ways to coexist in harmony
  As we all overcome many obstacles
  In hope to discover the simple purpose
  For our creation

Earth
Too dynamic to see all its diverse wonders
Yet, through the eyes of many cultures
We see visions of what our future beholds.

Earth
Too rich for one to hold the eminent vastness of its
    wealth
Yet, it provides to all more than enough resources
To sustain us for millenniums to come
Should we care for the child planet Earth
Within the greater universe.

JOURNEY OF THE DREAMER

I first came to know you as a child
When life was full of fun and smiles.
I chased you for miles and miles
Just to hold you for a little while.

I kept you in my heart and thoughts
Even when hope was nearly lost.
I saw glimpses of you pass my way
As we strayed apart on dreamless days.

I held you tight on lonely nights
With arms of truth as we took to flight.
Destined for places of limitless bound
Where dream and dreamer can only be found.

Remember the time when we took to sea;
Sailed its vastness and explored the depths.
From there we returned to green pastures to rest
Where we planned yet another quest.

Discovery is our homeland, we visited many times
    before.
So with courage to climb the highest peak we could find
We left the sheltered seasons where the four winds blow
To mold impressions from earthen matters gray within
    the mind.

So we tilled the soils from these fallow fields
To replenish the harvest fertile lands waste in haste
With grains of hope creations abundance yields
Sowed with seeds imagination hands create.

As we explore new horizons above
Launched thoughts that probe distant nebulas afar.
One constant element remains the same
Imagination's the path by which dream and dreamer
    came.

Order Form

Use this form to order additional copies of
Universal Reflections for your friends or family members.

Name:_____

Address:_____

City:_____State:_____Zip:_____

Daytime phone: (___)_____

If gift, message that you would like enclosed:

_____

_____

If gift, ship to:

Name:_____

Address:_____

City:_____State:_____Zip:_____

Method of payment: *(Make checks payable to Eggman Publishing, Inc.)*

❑ Check   ❑ Money order   ❑ VISA   ❑ MasterCard

Card #_____Exp._____

Signature:_____

(required for credit card purchases)

Quantity: _____ x $12.95 = $_____

Shipping & Handling Quantity: _____ x $3.00 = $_____

Subtotal: $_____

TN residents add 8.25% sales tax: $_____

TOTAL: $_____

Please return form and payment to
**Eggman Publishing, Inc.
3012 Hedrick St.,
Nashville, TN 37203.**

Thank you! Your order will shipped within 1–3 weeks from receipt.

FOR FASTER SERVICE CALL 1-800-396-4626

Order Form

Use this form to order additional copies of
Universal Reflections for your friends or family members.

Name:_____

Address:_____

City:_____State:_____Zip:_____

Daytime phone: (___)_____

If gift, message that you would like enclosed:

_____

_____

If gift, ship to:

Name:_____

Address:_____

City:_____State:_____Zip:_____

Method of payment: *(Make checks payable to Eggman Publishing, Inc.)*

❏ Check   ❏ Money order   ❏ VISA   ❏ MasterCard

Card #_____Exp._____

Signature:_____

(required for credit card purchases)

Quantity: _____ x $12.95 = $_____

Shipping & Handling Quantity: _____ x $3.00 = $_____

Subtotal: $_____

TN residents add 8.25% sales tax: $_____

TOTAL: $_____

Please return form and payment to
Eggman Publishing, Inc.
3012 Hedrick St.,
Nashville, TN 37203.

Thank you! Your order will shipped within 1–3 weeks from receipt.

FOR FASTER SERVICE CALL 1-800-396-4626